An American Song Book

A Collection of Original Songs

An American Song Book

A Collection of Original Songs

Published by Lulu Enterprises

67bullittmustang@gmail.com

www.lulu.com

Copyright 2016 - AL ALESSANDRA

Cover design by Lulu Enterprises, Inc. Interior images were copied from the internet and are constructed by the author as public domain. Other images are clip art. No other rights to images are claimed or implied by the author.

All rights reserved. No part of this publication may be reproduced or transmitted in any form or by any means, electronic, mechanical, photocopy, or recording, or any other retrieval system currently used or to be developed in the future, without the permission in writing from the author/copyright holder/publisher, except for brief quotations with respect to literary reviews.

ISBN:

Published in the United States of America

Printing/Distribution provided through:

Lulu Enterprises, Inc.

3131 RDU Center Dr., Ste. 210

Morrisville, NC 27560

An American Song Book

A Collection of Original Songs

by

AL ALESSANDRA

An American Song Book

INTRODUCTION

This book contains a collection of songs that I have written over the years. I believe there are recording artists in our country that are always looking for new songs to sing and record. I am hopeful that my contributions into this challenging area of creativity will offer prospective artists an opportunity to enhance their careers, by considering these original literary achievements.

Our country has never stood still when it came to creative, artistic, and cultural developments, especially, ventures into the musical arena.

I have always liked to write and have done so, my whole life, professionally and creatively.

I am hopeful and confident that I can contribute positively, through this new endeavor of mine and make a difference into somebody's career.

DEDICATION

This book is dedicated to my wife, Debbie, whose patience, encouragement, and extraordinary beauty, served as an inspiration to many of my songs; and to my entire family, which I believe is the most important aspect of my life.

TABLE OF CONTENTS

iv	Introduction
v	Dedication
Page 1-4	An American Legacy
Page 5-6	Beautiful
Page 7	Blackbird
Page 8-9	Broken Hearts
Page 10-11	Dreams at Night
Page 12-13	For My Love
Page 14-16	Gift of Love
Page 17-18	In the Beginning
Page 19-21	In Your Eyes
Page 22-24	In Your Eyes – Alternate Version
Page 25-26	Looking Away
Page 27-28	Looking for Love
Page 29-30	Love to You
Page 31-34	Love Tonight
Page 35-36	Loving You
Page 37-39	Night Dreams

TABLE OF CONTENTS

Page 40-41	Reachin' the End

Page 42-43	Sail Away

Page 44-45	Sailing

Page 46-47	When I Look in Eyes

Page 48-50	Whisper to Me

Page 51-53	Wish you Could See

Page 54-56	With You

Page 57-58	Words to You

Page 59-60	Words

Page 61-63	Young Man

Page 64-65	Your Eyes

Page 66-68	Your Love Never Dies

Page 69-70	You're the Best

Page 70-72	You're the One

An American Legacy

By Al Alessandra

There was a time in history in this great land of thee

When majestic mountains, high, rose o'er amber waves of grain

Long before the white man when the red man roamed so free

When teal blue streams reflected moonlight through the pines

But time is for eternity as history unwinds

As to this verdant country a land for freedom sought

Glistening streams they sailed and trails they left behind

Blood would flow so easily and many a battle fought

They came from lands so far away

Wind swept sails across the seas

They brought forth the visions of their day

This would prove to be a land born for liberty

Many fortunes won and lost-and many a debt to pay

Down the Missouri all through the Great Plains

But when winter time turned into the spring

The fur traders grew restless for hunting new game

Trappers blazed and tore up the trails

For they faced misfortune and despair

But for death n' drought they did not care

Through the night n' through the day

Where would they be sleeping tonight?

Where many Buffalo roamed so free and eagles soared in flight

A killing spree had no end in sight

Go west they said across this mighty land

The railroad men grew restless to hear the hammers sing

For here lies John Henry-steel drivin' man

They opened up the soil-the world at their command

Go west they said through the western stand

From sea to the sea-on native soil they tread

O'er mountain n' clear blue streams they spread

And forged the steel of industry

So many tears would flow

For many young men would come to see

They fought the wars to make men free

They fought for Manifest Destiny

For explorers, scouts, and cavalry too

They tread on lands of Cherokee, Cheyenne and Sioux

Go west they said, the earth stained red

For blood would flow-the Trail of Tears

A nation would divide on human misery

For a house divided can't stand alone

But in the end, a costly price that shaped our destiny

Across the great Rockies the rising sun would show

Shining down on waves of grain

Casting shadows a crimson glow

Spirits that touched the face of God

A short time for peace and harmony

A world at war, more lives were lost

For liberty and freedom sought

They sacrificed a deadly cost

But now we face a terrible foe

Across the shining sea they came

On native soil they tread to leave so many dead

Twin Towers fell, a terrible loss

We shall remember at any cost to prove our destiny

Rows of crosses lay silent now, for we shall not forget

Our American Legacy

Beautiful

By Al Alessandra

So many times I wonder
Now that I've found you
The magic in your eyes
I was meant to be here
And you were meant for me

I'll always be with you
Cause we've been through it all
I love you in my life for all times
I love you cause you're a friend of mine

Green eyes that light up the night
Your eyes, so warm, so real
I love the world your eyes reveal

So I say to you, you're beautiful tonight
I know that you'll never leave-can't you see
Cause you believe in me
The way I believe in you
Loving you is so easy to do

Oh, it's true
You're beautiful, tonight?
I was meant to be here
And you were meant for me
You know that I'll never change
Cause we've been through it all, you n' me
For such a long, long time

I've got to say you'll be mine
Right down the line
I'm so lucky to be here, shinning bright
You're so beautiful, tonight

BLACKBIRD

By Al Alessandra

Blackbird rise, Blackbird rise

Eyes glimmering through the night

Blackbird fly, into the wind of the early light

Blackbird cry

You're always searching for some company

Blackbird cry

You won't be lonely tonight, can't you see

Blackbird fly

Blackbird fly, you're gonna be free tonight

Blackbird fly

On the wings of the morning light

Broken Hearts

By Al Alessandra

It was a cold September day

When our love went astray

Don't know why you left me this way

Many times I've lost my way

But a broken heart knows...Oh

Chorus

So, where do broken hearts go?

Is there a special place, you know

When you lose your heart and soul

Like I did when I lost you

Will I find my way there?

Don't tell me it's true
That our love is through
Will I find my way there?
Back to where our hearts glow
Is there a special place to go?
To find our love again
Where warm winds blow
And the sun shines bright

Chorus

So, tell me where to find our love
Like the promise of morning light
So, I can find my way tonight
And be together don't you know
Before, with hearts aglow
For I'll love you, forever more

Chorus 2x

Dreams at Night

By Al Alessandra

Dreams surround me

The winds of time pass me by

There are dreams that I want to see

But as long as you believe in me

It doesn't matter anymore

Dreaming my life away

Dreams pass me by

Monday blues always bring me down

But your love was meant for me

And I'll never ever set you free

Like restless waves to the shores
I'll be here once more
The dreams of life, the dreams of life
The dreams at night go on and on

Gentle voices I hear
Now I'm beginning to see
Where life is leading me
Cause I'm dreamin' of loving you

Dreams will set me free
But now I've got to find my way
Like endless waves to the shores
I'll love you forever more

The dreams of life, the dreams of life
Dreams of love are fading by and by
The dreams of life, the dreams of life

For My Love

By Al Alessandra

You know I love you so

My life is new again

Friends ask me why

I explain it all in a sigh

Beauty not seen before

They just don't understand

My love is forever more

Loneliness is a sad affair

Shadows surround me

But no one will bring me down

Now that I'm around you

You say you love me too
Your love was meant to be
Like a soft summer breeze
You put my soul at ease

Loneliness is a sad affair
Shadows surround me
But no one will bring me down
Now that I'm around you

Gift of Love

By Al Alessandra

Whatever will be will be
They say it's destiny
I was looking for love, so desperately
So, you gave me the gift of love
The gift of love

Heaven only knows
Your love was sent from above
Beauty I've missed so many times before
But now that I've found you
There's nothing else you can do

Nothing you can say
I see it in your eyes
But it's the right thing to do
Darling, color my world
With the gift of love
The color of love-is the gift of love
The gift of love

Your love surrounds me
Now that I've found you, babe
You gave me a gift that's like
A gift from above

I know how lonely life can be
Shadows follow me
But, your love will set us free
You gave me the gift of love
The gift of love

Darling, can't you see

I was meant to be here

And you were made for me

Oh, you gave me the gift of love

The gift of love

Darling, show me the way

To the gift of love

The gift of love

In the Beginning

By Al Alessandra

In my own time

Life was unkind

And sometimes it's blind

But now it's so clear, why we are here

You were made for me-it's only the beginning

It doesn't matter at all

So, I say to you

You were meant to be here, with me

Forever and free

There were things I said

I shouldn't have said

But whatever will be, will be

You made it so clear how fate could define

We were meant to be here-from the beginning

It's no surprise

That life is unkind

And sometimes it's blind

But it's clear can't you see

You were sent to me

So can you explain?

How fate could define

Why we we're here

It doesn't matter at all

You were meant to be, with me, from the beginning

In Your Eyes

By Al Alessandra

You've been on my mind for such a long time

Always, when I wake up with a song

Beauty in your eyes

Like the dawn's early light

In your eyes

I love the way you smile

Bless my soul

Can you stay with me a while

In peaceful dreams I see

I love your style

Stay with me awhile

In your eyes

I need your love to last

Now that I've found you

You chased away the shadows of my past

In your eyes

You're the only one I see

Please tell me?

Do you feel the same way, too?

In your eyes

The doorway till the end of time

You give me peace of mind

Bless my soul

Your love is gonna shine

In your eyes

I love the way you smile

Stay with me a while

You're the only one for me

Heaven knows

I'm gonna be with you

Till the end of time

In Your Eyes
Alternate Version
By Al Alessandra

You've been on my mind for such a long time

Always, when I wake up with a song

In your eyes

That light up with the dawn

Your eyes

I love the way you smile

Bless my soul

Can you stay with me a while

Wondering through the night

I see you when I wake up with the dawn

Your eyes

I need your love to last

Now that I've found you

You chased away the shadows of my past

Your eyes

You're the only one I see

Your eyes

Please tell me?

Do you feel the same way, too?

Your eyes

Like the dawn's early light

You give me peace of mind

Heaven only knows

I'm gonna love you, till the end of time

Your eyes

I love the way you smile

Stay with me a while

You're the only one for me

Heaven knows-can't you see

I'm gonna be with you

Till the end of time

Looking Away

By Al Alessandra

Don't you wonder somehow?

When life reaches out

It's not what it seems to be

Shadows casting a veil

As the night closes in

So we just pass them by

Misfortune and despair

As they stand there alone
Through the day 'n night
Signs in the blazing light
Homeless and hungry they say
So much sadness and despair
As we look away and stare
For they too had dreams so bright
But we close our eyes
As we pass them by
And pretend not to see
What life must really be?
For pain and suffering
As we look away and join
The ones who care not for others
Into the dawning light
They'll be no twists of fate
If we look away in the night
With a heart of stone
For they too had dreams so bright

Looking for Love

By Al Alessandra

Can you really tell me?
Why we carry on this way?
Looking for love to stay

Searching for reasons
That never comes our way
We're lost in the games we play

Are we afraid to say?
We'll never find a way
Of staying close together
Everyday

Loving you was right
Every night
But now I realize
Words got in the way

Understanding but
Not realizing why
We're so far away
I need your love to stay

Thoughts of losing you
Rush through me
But disappear
When I look in your eyes

We could start anew
But that's so hard to do
When you're lost
In the games we play

Love to You

By Al Alessandra

I know I love you

I'm really sure that I do

I like you just the way you are

A sense of happiness I feel

Like a shooting star

Like a burst of spring

I'm feeling something new

Something warm and true

Do you feel the same way too?

Because I'm learning about you

Like glowing sunshine when a new day comes through

I know that I love you

I like you just the way you are

Do you love me too?

Do you...do you...?

LOVE TONIGHT

By Al Alessandra

So long ago-I can't remember when, it was such a long n' lonely night

That's when I met my only friend

If you want it better, you've got to do it better

Let's pull it all together

I'm driving hard tonight

With you in my sights

I've seen the sun rising through the early mornin' dawn

Fate is what they always say

It was cold but I've got to carry on some way

Like chasing clouds away

We're caught up in this human race

She had such a pretty face

I wondered how I found this crazy place

Chorus:

Hey, hey, hey, if you want it better

You've got to do it better

Life is not forever

Make your life worth living

Cause things will be alright

In the middle of this madness

We can drive it hard tonight

Love will always be in sight

She was alone

It was a cold November day

We can't let our love slip away

But there's got to be another way

Somewhere on this street of dreams

We'll find a way for new love

In a world gone astray

So many thoughts surround me

Telling me that love will find its way

A twist of fate-do you believe, in what they say

On this cold November day

Love will always find its way-hey...

[Chorus:]

This place is cold-it was a dark December day

I need to break away from this charade

But there's got to be a better way

Can't live life day by day

In a maze of ugliness and greed

Blazing clouds a violet haze

This world has changed but I can stay the same

Dark hotels, cheap wine n' cigarettes

So many fortunes won and lost

Good news, bright lights n' dying dreams

But somewhere in this crazy place

I've found you and found some sanity

Cause you n' me we'll see the light

For our love was meant to be

We can drive it hard tonight

With you in my sights

Loving You

By Al Alessandra

There's nothing' that makes me feel this way

Nothing' else I can do

So, make my dreams come true, babe

Cause' loving' you's the only thing to do

It's the only thing, so true

True love's so hard to find

No one can save your love but me, babe

It's time to see I'm the only one for you

Loving' you's the only thing to do

It's the only thing, so true

Loving you was easy

Like a river flowing a little too free

But I'm with you now and love is here to stay

I knew this would be my day

I want you in my life for all times

You make me feel so fine, babe

Cause' I feel the magic with you

Loving' you's the only thing to do

It's the only thing to do

There's nothing' that can keep me away

My love will never stray, babe

Set your love in motion

Show me your emotions

Cause' I'm in love with you, babe

Oh, I'm so in love with you

(Repeat and fade away)

Night Dreams

By Al Alessandra

Dreams that arouse me

Never seeming to end

A world that surrounds me

I can't understand

Words that I've said

I shouldn't have said

Beauty not seen

In my life before

Feelings for you

Will be there in the end
I'll always defend thee
For what the truth is
No one understands
Cause I love you...
Yes I love you
Ohhh how I love you

Notions fill my head
From people around me
Just how I feel about you
They can't understand
No sense in this world anymore
The truth I'm searching for
Thoughts I can't understand
Just what I want to be
I will be in the end

Cause I love you...
Yes I love you
Ohhh how I love you

Dreams that arouse me

Never seeming to end

A world that surrounds me

I can't understand

Words that I've said

I shouldn't have said

Beauty not seen

In my life before

Feelings for you

Will be there in the end

I'll always defend thee

For what the truth is

No one understands

Cause I love you...

Yes I love you

Ohhh... How I love you

Reachin' the End

By Al Alessandra

Ooh, ooh ooh, ooh…Ooh ooh ooh, ooh

Hey, it's time to take this badge off of me

I won't need it anymore

You see I'm reachin' the end

It's a mad world can't you see

Heaven only knows the reality for me

I'm reachin' the end now

My life's clear to see

They try to take these guns from me

But I don't see that cause I'm free

Now I'm reachin' heaven's door

Darkness shrouding over me

But I can see it's not too dark for me

So believe in me

I'm gonna be free

Ooh ooh ooh, ooh ooh ooh

Sail Away

By Al Alessandra

Sailing

Sail away with me

Let's slip away in the morning light

We can find serenity

Sailing

Sail away with me

And if the wind is right we'll drift all night

We can find some harmony

Sailing

Sail away with me

It makes me feel so fine

Just like a melody

Come with me and sail away

Sail away with me

For you will see

Reality, for you n' me

Sailing

By Al Alessandra

Sailing

Sail away with me

Let's slip away in the glimmering light

And find serenity

Sailing

Sail away with me

And if the wind is right we'll drift all night

And find some harmony

Sailing

Sail away with me

It makes you feel so fine

Just like a melody

Come sail away with me

Cause we're gonna find

Serenity for you n' me

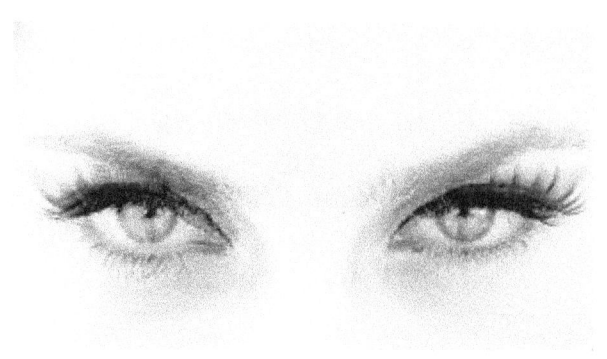

When I look in Your Eyes

By Al Alessandra

When I look in your eyes

I see the magic of the stars in your eyes

Reflections of glimmering light

As I look into your eyes, I realize

I see the deepness of the sea in your eyes

In your eyes

I see the deepness of the love in your eyes

And it's no surprise; I see the color of love in your eyes

The love I feel you have for me

When I look into your eyes

I see the beauty of no other in your eyes
And when we're alone
They'll be no tears, no goodbyes
I'll just look into your eyes,
Tenderly

Your eyes, so warm, so real
I'll love you in my life, for all time
When I look into your eyes

Whisper to Me

By Al Alessandra

Come with me if you please

Set your mind in motion

Remember how it used to be

Show me your emotions

Reminiscing through the years

I'll always defend thee

I will be there by your side

We must be together

I'll make a fire's glow

To keep you warm in winter

Yellow roses by your side

To give you in December

I will be there when you call

Set your mind in motion

I will be, you will see

I will not forsake thee

I will be there by your side

We must be together

Whisper softly, let's come through

Whisper for love, so true

It doesn't matter at all

I'll be there when you call

What will be, will be

Ain't always so

Seeing is believing

True love will find a way

Many things in life are free

I will not deceive thee

I will be, you will see

We must be together

Come to me, run to me

Say you love me too

It doesn't matter to me

Chasing the clouds away

My love is here to stay

So, come with me if you please

Set your mind in motion

I will be, you will see

We must be together

Come with me if you please

I will not forsake thee

I will be there by your side

We must be together

We must be together

Wish you Could See

By Al Alessandra

So

So you're gonna tell me

You're trading your life

For a life made in hell

You're trading good friends

For those who deceive you

A smile from one who sells

Who pretends to be true

Did they get you to trade?

Your soul to get high

Did you think you could find

Friends you left behind

Did you then realize?

A cruel world

When you opened your eyes

And finally realized

You traded your soul

For a world of lies

Now I wish

How I wish you could see

We're just two souls that should be

Together, day after day

In this crazy world
Now that you've found
That same old love
Love meant for you n' me
Wish you could see

With You

By Al Alessandra

My life is worth living

Forget what they say

Wonderin' how I made it

Bless my soul, with you by my side

Keep your loving in stride

When the blues keep coming

You gotta make a new day

That's what I say

You've gotta turn it around

Turn it around

With a song, a new day
Don't worry my friend,
Gonna love you till the end
You can do it, I say
Good times I'd be living
Chasin' those blues away
Anytime I get lonely
With you by my side
Our love will abide

Gotta lifetime to share
Cause I'll always be there
Gotta take it in stride
Your love is like a song in the night
Whatever is done, is done
It doesn't matter at all
I'll be there when you call

Grew up believin'
The father, son and Holy Ghost
A world of believers
But what matters the most
What will be in the end
Like a song in the night
Cause you're my best friend

For my life is worth living
With you by my side
Well find some harmony
When those blues keep callin'
You gotta take it in stride
Seeing is believing
With you by my side

You gotta turn it around
You can do it my friend
And turn it around
Turn it around

Words to You

By Al Alessandra

I've said so many things

In my life to you

But through it all

Good times we've shared

But we're together now

So please listen to me

I know what you think of me

Is what I'd like to be

I've treated you unkindly

But can't you see

No one means so much to me

The truth you tried to show me

But I was too blind to see

You stood up to me

And I just waked away

But now I'm so much better

So my thoughts should come together

Just like a melody

Our love was meant to be

I love you in a world

Where there's no end of time

For in my life

You gave me peace of mind

And when my life is over

Remember what we shared together

I believe in you, so believe in me

My love is forever more

Repeat verse 3

We're together now and

I'm giving my love to you

WORDS

By Al Alessandra

Stunning, caring, warm and tender
These are words that describe her
Graceful, slender, a face to remember
Easier by far it is
To find your way in dreams
Than to find the words to describe her
Carefree, easy, bright and breezy
A sentimental lover
There are no words to discover
These are the words

Easier by far it is
To find your way
Than to find the words to describe her

Carefree, easy, bright and breezy
Always a sentimental lover
There are no words to discover
So beautiful is what I say
Of the beauty inside her
Where are the words
These are the words

Young Man

By Al Alessandra

Young man look at me now

I was once what you are

Young man look at me now

I was once what you are

Young man look what I've done

Sixty four, forever more

And in the end there's so much more

Lived life that passed me by

Where did they all go?

Lived life and loved by some

Regrets I had a few

But through it all

I'll tell some things to you
Young man look at me now
I was once like you are
Love, love, too hard to find
Is it the same for you?
If you can read my mind
You'll know it's true

Sunshine makes me feel so fine
I've been around this world, so new
Just what I'm going through
I just can't understand

I've won some and lost a few
Wondering where the years slipped through
Someday you'll be there too
Young man look at me now
I was once like you are
Love, too hard to find
Is it the same for you?
If you can read my mind

You'll know it's true

Young man look at me now

I was once what you are

Young man look at me now

I was once what you are

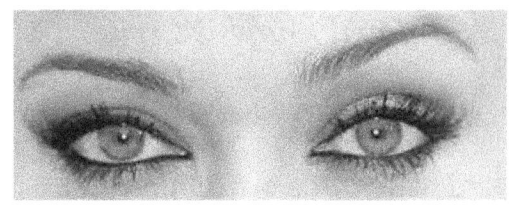

Your Eyes

By Al Alessandra

Nights surround me, never seeming to end

Dreams arouse me, endless thoughts in my head

Beauty I always see when I look in your eyes

Just what I'm going through, I'm beginning to see

Cause I love you, yes I do, do you love me too?

When I look in your eyes

I see the love your eyes reveal

The love I feel you feel for me

Cause I love you

Yes I love you

Do you love me too?

Beauty I always see when I look in your eyes

Truth in a world, I don't see anymore

Darkness around us, I can't understand

But I love you

Oh how I love you

Do you love me too?

Your Love Never Dies

By Al Alessandra

Darling I'm lost

My heart is bleeding on the floor

Waiting to see you again

Oh, what a thrill it is

When you walk through that door

I cry out for more

Like waves rushing to the shores

I'll love you forever more

{Chorus :}

Until the day

Until the day fades away

Until there's no more good-byes

When you say you're mine

Beauty in your eyes

Your love never dies

Darling you're the one

Just like the rising sun

Make me the only one

In the name of love

I won't be outdone

Every night

Your love is here to stay

Even though you're far away

Come with me-lay with me

Don't let your love stray away

Let your love shine through

Cause you'll always be mine

Till the end of time

Chorus

Until the day...

You're the Best

By Al Alessandra

No one looks better than you

It's really true, babe

Beauty not seen before

Cause no one looks quite as good as you

Baby, you're the best

There I was lost and alone

Loneliness-I always knew

But then I found you

My searching's through

Heaven only knows

There'll be no sharing tonight

Just let your love life flow

Cause no one looks quite as good as you

When I hold you tight

There's so much to say

What kind of magic made you this way?

Heaven only knows

I only have love for you

Just let your love life flow

No one looks better than you

It's really true, babe

Beauty not seen before

Cause no one looks quite as good as you

Baby, you're the best

You're the One

By Al Alessandra

I saw you standing there
Waves rushing to the shore
Beauty I'd dreamed of
So many times before

Maybe this time
Love will find a way
For loneliness follows me
Will your love be true?

When reality climbs up inside
I'll love you the whole day through
Like dawning sunshine for you n' I
Oh baby, you're the one

No shadows surround me
Forbidden love so many times before
It doesn't matter to me
Chasing the clouds away

For loneliness is always there
It's there until you find someone
Now that I've found you
Baby you're the one

www.ingramcontent.com/pod-product-compliance
Lightning Source LLC
Chambersburg PA
CBHW080601090426
42735CB00016B/3310